The 3-Day Business Cleanse:

How to Get the Sh*t Out of Your Business
and Get Things Moving Again

Jenny Thompson

Table of Contents

Introduction

People who meet me frequently introduce me as one of the best marketers they have ever met. Now whether you think that's a compliment or an insult, that's up to you. But even if I'm one of the best marketers, the truth is that for a very long time, I was one of the worst leaders. And in fact, I would say I wasn't even a bad leader, I was a bad manager. I might even go one step further and say that I was so bad at whatever it was, I wouldn't call myself a leader or a manager. Early in my career I was managing one assistant and what seemed like overnight, I got an opportunity to take over a business that had 20 plus employees, only one of whom I had ever met. I had a very short transition, I had no mentor, and while I respected my boss, I had no examples of what good *leadership* was. So I defaulted to what so many of us default to, which is this "idea" of being the boss. I was going to make decisions and I was going to be firm and I was going to be in charge. I did all of that, and I did really insane things like deciding I had to have a certain parking spot in order to be the most important person in my business. I once yelled at somebody from another division because he was using paper that my division had paid for. In an illustration of how bad a manager I was, I quickly decided that the only way to protect my division's paper budget, was to keep the paper in my office. My office was locked every night, as if there was some big paper stealing ring that was going on behind our backs in the evenings. When I left for a business trip, I did it with all the paper locked inside my office. Now you can imagine, because of how rude and cheap and unprofessional I had been about paper, when my team needed paper, the other divisions were not exactly lining up to lend it to us.

Unfortunately that wasn't the day I learned the lesson. But I did learn it a year or so later.

What's that lesson? It's that your office and your parking spot and your job title, do not make you a leader. They make you a person who has a parking spot, and an office and a title. You can be the most horrible person with those, or you can be a person of quality, but they aren't what make you either of those things. It has to come from inside you. One of the things that you have to remember as a leader, is that everyone is looking to you at all times. They are looking to you for examples on how to act in the workplace. They are looking to you for examples of good business decisions, and they are looking to you for examples on how to treat other people and how to interact with other people. That is why so often we see these horrible generations of leadership at large companies, because people copy what they learn. We know it's true in family units. We see that people who have challenging home lives grow up and create challenging environments for their children. Why would we think it's any different at work? In fact, in a lot of cases we spend more time with the people at work and surrounded by the people at work then we do at home, so we have to recognize that people are always looking to us. They are always watching what we do.

The day that I woke up was actually Christmas day. I had a tradition of going for a movie and Chinese food with my sister, but it was the year that her son was born, and she wasn't available for a movie or Chinese food. I ended up reading a book by John Maxwell, who is one of the most brilliant and inspirational leadership leaders that I know of. I read this book called "The 21 Irrefutable Laws of Leadership: Follow them and people will follow you." This was the first book that changed my life. And, as it turned out, it changed the lives of my current and future employees – whether they realized it or not.

I realized—and this is my metaphor, not his, (I don't want people to blame him if they don't think it's effective)— I was driving a bus and there were two or three people who were sitting in the front row or the front two rows and they could kind of see where they were going, but they were still completely at my mercy. I would stop and start. I could turn whenever I wanted and they were just there for the ride. As you go further back, the people couldn't even see where we were headed. So they have no concept, they are just on the bus. If they want to get off the bus, they don't know when they are going to be able to get off. If they need something, they don't know what they are going to need. That was a great metaphor for how I was running my business. I was in charge. I was the boss. I was going to make decisions. If I thought it was a good idea, we would do it. If I thought it was a bad idea, we wouldn't. I had my handful of people that were on my leadership team that would be right there with me, and they were the ones that would basically go to the "minions" and say, "This is what we were going to do." It was a great illustration for me.

After I got back from that Christmas vacation, I called my team together and I told them, "I have been a terrible leader to you. I have focused on all the wrong things. I have given you poor examples of leadership and I hope that you'll forgive me. I hope that you'll give me another chance to be the kind of the leader that you deserve."

I spent a lot of time working on improving the way I lead a business. In some ways, that is about your personal relationships with your team. In some ways it's about the business that you run, how you structure it, what you do with it. And in most ways, it's about how you make a decision and the willingness to make a decision.

Along the way, when I got to this point, I realized I had made a lot of very bad decisions and I had failed to make important decisions. My business had a lot of aspects to it that were not positive. There were a lot of employees that I had adopted who I probably never would have hired on my own, but they were just part of it now. There were people that were in positions where they probably weren't able to use their strengths as well as they could have. There were business units that weren't contributing value.

I was running a natural medicine business and we were publishing health newsletters. We actually had doctors who we were working with who would call and scream at the employees. I had one doctor that I think 5 or 6 employees had come into my office crying after talking to him. This was not a way that the business should run. So, the reason I developed this process was to take time at least once a year to look at the business, to look at the areas that were holding it up. To look at the talent that we weren't tapping into and to look at the people who weren't in the right positions and maybe shouldn't be a part of the company anymore. To streamline the business and make it work as effectively as possible. That meant focusing on the projects that had great opportunity for us. It meant being willing to kill the projects that didn't. I had to restructure the business to ensure we were taking advantage of the talents and interests and energy of the people that were going to move us forward and make the very honest and difficult decisions to identify the people that couldn't move us forward, and develop an exit strategy for them.

Today I am a much better leader. I make mistakes every single day. I'm very upfront and honest about them with my team. And when I do this, I have rules for how I admit my failures and deal with them. I admit them very publicly because I think it's important for your team to see that you can fail and still succeed. It's important to me and the business for them to emulate that behavior. I left the company where I learned all these wonderful lessons after almost 20 years, and I started my own tech company.

It is a very different world. I no longer have inventory and product costs. I'm no longer marketing in a direct-to-consumer single sale situation. I'm building a tech company that I expect to be something that will be on everybody's lips in three years. Being in startup mode is very different than running a $70 million-dollar business with 1.2 million customers and 15 to

18 different business units. But the thing that's the same is that I use the same decision-making strategies. I use the same way of evaluating whether something can positively impact my business enough that we should do it. I continue to lead my team in a way that I know I'm in charge, the decisions have to be mine, but the way that we make decisions, the way that we focus the business is all together and that the team understands why we are doing things even if they are not part of the actual decision-making process.

Chapter 1: How will a Business Cleanse Benefit You?

So what will the process do for you? Why should you do a 3-day business cleanse with your team? The first thing is, you'll get unstuck. If you are part of a mature business, you have things in your business like I did--that are just kind of chugging along while you are kind of stuck in that same place. This is a great opportunity to move out of that feeling of 'stuckness.' It also lets you streamline your business for maximum profitability. To look at the areas where maybe you are overspending or you are not getting enough profit or products that you are keeping on life support. I used to have a saying that, "We are not in the product resuscitation business," and so these products that can't sustain themselves have to be terminated. This is a way to identify those and to figure out how to exit from those business units or those products. You'll also get to identify your best and most committed team members, and make sure that you are giving them the biggest opportunities and matching the opportunities to their skill set. You'll prioritize the opportunities for your business by actual opportunities.

Success Story

One client that hired me to take them through the Cleanse was a $20 million-dollar business and they were stuck at that $20 million mark for a few years. In an attempt to bust through it, the owner of the company decided to launch another business unit that really had nothing to do with the core competencies of the company. Let's just say for discretion's sake, that the company was making flavored water and now they were going to start making ballpoint pens. Everybody on the team came in and they loved the idea of working for a flavored water company and then, all of a sudden, he wants them to make ballpoint pens. None of them wanted to do it. But this was something that he was very passionate about. He thought this was the best ballpoint pen. He believed everyone who loved the water would want to use the same pen he was using. As we went through this process, he understood that the profitability opportunity wasn't there. It was going to distract his best people from building the flavored water business and, even though he saw the connection, his customers didn't. His customers came to him for something very specific and they didn't really believe that he was the right person to have this other business relationship with. During that meeting, we were able to streamline the business and shut down the unit that the team did not feel passionate about. Everyone was relieved. The team didn't know how to sell it and it was distracting them from their core business.

Success Story

With a different client, we had a "scagull" problem with one of the editors. If you don't know what a seagull problem is, it's somebody who swoops in every once in a while, shits all over everything and then flies away. So here was somebody, they were using his name and relationship with the readers to promote the newsletter. And as the editor, he was responsible for the approving the content but he was frequently unavailable. They weren't able to get steady enough communication from him or steady enough content from him and then they would put something together and he would come in and say, "This is horrible, don't you dare put my name on it," and then he would fly off.

We talked about whether they should terminate the relationship, but everyone agreed he was a valuable asset. So, after reviewing all the options through the 3-day Cleanse, we developed an entire new strategy for who would communicate with him, how they would communicate with him, and what they would do in advance. It let him be as uninvolved in the day-to-day of the business as he wanted to be but feel much better about the content that was being put out, and move out of the monthly content review. It was a perfect solution, where they still got to benefit from his name and reputation and he still got to build a relationship with the customers, but they didn't go into this frenzy every time he got the editorial to review.

Figuring out which opportunities should be focused on, how to refocus on those opportunities and how to get the maximum benefit from your productive business units is are the core advantages of this process. However, another benefit is that you'll identify who your "C" players are and you'll develop exit strategies for them. Now some people are very uncomfortable saying, "If the person is not contributing to the business, they are going to have to leave." Firing is a very hard thing for most people. If you decide you don't want to fire somebody, you will at least be honest about what their weaknesses are and move them to a position that uses their strengths in the greatest way.

The other thing this process will do is identify which of your employees you may be uncomfortable leading. Relationship dynamics are challenging. And being the leader doesn't mean you can't be intimidated by an employee. Identifying this and developing strategies for it helps you resume your position of leadership in a comfortable, non-confrontational way.

I was working with a client and there was one employee who was from another culture and was much bolder than the owners of the company. Essentially, this person decided to take over all of operations. They had made them the Customer Service Manager, he end up taking over all the operations without their agreement. In doing that, he essentially bullied them into doing things the way that he wanted. We were able to, in this process, identify where his strengths were, identify where he had over stepped and developed a plan for him to take over a very specific business unit so that he could run something that tapped into his strengths, but not interact with people that the owners didn't want him to interact with and not continue to put them in a vulnerable position where he was running core parts of the business that they couldn't run without him. That was kind of a way for them to start the discussion of an exit without being committed to an exit. or without having to make a sudden change that they thought would negatively impact the rest of the team and particularly the people that reported to him.

Chapter 2: What's the downside of not doing a Business Cleanse?

The first risk of not taking the time for this process is over-investing in projects and products with limited opportunity. Investing too much money, investing too much marketing capital, and/or investing too much personnel. Any time you are investing in projects and products that can't build up your company, you are taking a double hit. You are losing potential opportunity and you are getting much lower return on all those resources. Not just for today, but for the future. It's at least a double whammy – maybe a triple.

The other downside is keeping employees too long and then seeming heartless when you let them go. Sometimes it's worse and you just decide not to let them go. You end up paying people who aren't contributing to your business. You end up letting them get more and more ingratiated with your team until it's harder and harder to let them go. This is especially true if you are a small business owner or it's your own business. Literally every dollar you put in somebody's pocket who does not move your company forward is a dollar you are taking away from yourself, your most valued employees, or your marketing budget. So again, you are not just not growing, you are actually hindering your growth by stealing money from things that could grow your business and investing it in people who can't.

Another downside is you will keep feeling stuck and uninspired. Remember at the beginning, when you would go into your office every day and think, "Oh my God, we could do this and this and this! And maybe we'll test this. And then we will make more of these!" You were full of excitement and thrilled to build the business. But when you don't have that passion for your business anymore, everything is just a little bit less productive, somewhat less profitable, and a lot less exciting. When revenues or profits start to fall and you have to find a way to replace them, you are not in the position to do it because you haven't been looking at your business the same way. You'll also have an unhappy and unfulfilled team -- and that can breed disloyalty and create bad morale. If people feel engaged, excited, if they know that you will kill the projects no one believes in and that aren't bringing value , and if they know that you will listen to them about the things they do want to build with you, they feel so much more valuable, and that actually creates more value for your company. Happy committed workforces are the most important asset in any organization.

I wish I had developed —and used -- the Business Cleanse sooner. I shared with you what a terrible manager I was early in my career. Because of that, I lost a lot of talented people. Not only by being a jerk, but by not focusing on the right challenges for them and the right opportunities. I just thought, "This is your job, get on this hamster wheel and go, go, go." I didn't stop and think, "Here's what you are great at. Here is what I see that you don't like to do, let's see if there is another opportunity for you." I was just a horrible manager and a horrible leader, and people didn't want to work with me or for me for a long time.

It makes you settle for people who aren't as good, because your top people are leaving and you can't afford to lose everybody. It also lets business units drag on that should be shut down sooner. They eventually peter out and at the end, people are ignoring them. There is no value and sometimes the customers don't even like the product anymore because you are not putting the same amount of attention into it. These things just shouldn't be connected to your brand anymore, but they stay for way too long.

I also know I missed out on some valuable opportunities by not being open enough to change. Now, I was always happy to be second. I never felt the need to be the pioneer in something. If somebody in my business hasn't made it work, I don't feel the need to be the first one. I think that's best illustrated with some of the online marketing opportunities. All the people that placed ads on Facebook when you couldn't market in the newsfeed and could only ads on the side lost money. I kept sitting back and saying, "When somebody figures this out, I'll be ready to dive in. But I haven't figured it out and I know people are losing money doing this."

But I think about the things that I was just stubborn about -- "This is our standard model," I would think. I wasn't willing to be the first or second or third one to dive in. I kept saying, "Nobody is making money on that. Nobody is making money on that." And people are saying, "Are you kidding? People are making so much money on this." I know people who launched entire businesses on Instagram or Pinterest, while I was still very focused on this one model of email marketing that we were doing.

I also wish I had started with the Business Cleanse sooner because I built out a lot of valuable personal and professional connections that I learned a lot from as I did this. Once I started looking at where the opportunities were that were outside of my company, I had to reach out to people. I learned so much and made close friends. I wish I had understood the deep, long-term benefits of networking and start it a lot sooner.

Lastly, the other reason I wish I had made the Cleanse part of my business practice earlier is that it's can be difficult and complex to undo something that isn't working. It is always simple to just not start it in the first place or to cut it off early. It's a bit like a golf swing. When I took golf lessons, the instructor asked me, "How long have you been playing?" I said, "Oh, I haven't been playing. My husband wants me to learn so he bought me these lessons." And this guy had this "Thank you, God" look on his face. He was so thrilled that he was going to get to work with somebody who didn't have a lot of mistakes he needed to correct. It's very hard to unteach a bad golf swing. Well that's how I feel about clogging up your business with a lot of things it doesn't need. It is so much easier if you do this process regularly and you either identify the projects you shouldn't even start on, or you are weeding them out so regularly that they don't become part of this big blob that you can't get rid of.

So, if you are feeling stuck. If you are settling for good enough, like the business is just there and it's 'fine.' And if you are f bored and if you have employees that you know you are not working at the best of their ability or you've just been kind of keeping around because you are not sure what to do with them, then it is time for a 3-Day Cleanse.

Maybe you're concerned about the outcome. Your key people might feel threatened. "We are going to make a lot of changes, what does this mean for me?" You might be worried that your pet project is going to be exposed as not being something valuable. Or that things are working just fine and you don't want to risk the profits. Or maybe it's because it's Christmas, or Thanksgiving, or New Year's or Memorial Day and it's just not a good time for those kinds of changes right now. Then I promise you this, even doing one chunk of the process will help. You don't have to commit to the entire thing, but just start. It's just like if you want to get healthy, but you don't want to do a 5-day fast. If you just do one green juice in the morning instead of having a cinnamon bun, that is still progress. So let's do the one green juice commitment and then we'll see how we go from there.

Chapter 3: Planning your 3-Day Business Cleanse

First, a quick overview of the three steps of the process:

1) Unpack
2) Dissect and Destroy
3) Brainstorm and Rebuild

I know destroy sounds scary, but one of the things that I can't emphasize enough is that we aren't here to just make minor changes. We aren't here to put stuff on the "back burner," or to take a to-do list of 112 things and move number 82 up to the number 17 slot. We are here to streamline your business to let you focus on the things that are going to create the most opportunity possible. To let you stop getting distracted by things that are never going to build your business. To do that, we have to destroy some things. We are going to build it better and stronger than it is today.

I've already shared with you why to do it. You are going to do it because it's going to make your business better. It's going to make you a better leader. It's going to let your team see where you are going. It's going to open up the vision of that bus ride, and it's going to keep you focused on the best way to move your business forward and let you get rid of your distractions.

Why 3 days? It's important that it's all done at the same time. And it can't all be done in a day. We are using a lot of different parts of the brain in this, and it's important that you get to stopping points and you let your brain refresh and recharge.

The location and the team are extremely important for the success of this.

Location

This is critical: It should not be in your office. It should not be in the conference room downstairs from your office. Rent an offsite location that is easy for everyone on your team to get to. You don't have to go to Fiji, you can go to the Hilton downtown, but you have to be offsite. It's too easy for people to distract you when they can walk in and they can interrupt you at any minute. It's also too easy for your people to go back to their desks and get distracted answering emails. This is a very important and focused process and it is critical that this is the number one priority for everybody who is participating. Not to mention you will be having sensitive conversations about the business that you may not want overheard.

The other thing about the location is that it has to have windows. You cannot do this in a dark, closed room. It will not benefit the process. Make sure that people can see what's going on outside.

Plan to have snacks throughout and have lunch brought in from somewhere different all three days. Getting in a routine over the days will interfere with the creativity requires for the process.

Choosing the right facilitator

It's very important that you have a facilitator that is not one of your team members and it is not the CEO. Anyone you trust who is capable to controlling a meeting can do this. You can bring in somebody that you worked with as a consultant on something else. If you work for a large company that has several different business units, as long as somebody is not part of your business in any direct way, you can bring them in.

Here's the catch: The facilitator must have nothing to lose and no long-term involvement in your business. When I do this professionally, I do it as a three-day window and I never accept long term commitments from people that I work with. I need to be able to be completely candid in that room. I need to be able to say that this project needs to be killed. That the CEO was focused on the wrong things. That this person should be fired (although that's a private conversation in another room). If I am setting myself up for a long-term commitment, if I'm basically in there as a sales pitch, I am not going to be as candid as I need to be to get the best results. So, somebody who is looking for a monthly retainer as a consultant is not the person who should facilitate this. It also needs to be somebody who will call "BS," who will stop a conversation, who will say, "That is not what you said yesterday. I think you are being soft on this thing." It's critical while they are respectful to everybody in the room, that they are in charge and still making sure the conversation is honest and headed in the right direction. Also, they must be willing to stop a conversation that is unproductive. A lot of times people will just let things drone on and on and on and on. I can't tell you how many times in my career I have said, "I'm going to end this conversation. You guys can revisit it later if you'd like, but it's no longer contributing to this meeting so we are moving on from it." They have to be willing to say that in a room full of people.

Who to include

There should be no more than 7 people from your team in the room. The absolute top leadership should be there every day and the other people should rotate. I think it's very important to have people who talk directly to your customers when you are talking about the business, but they probably shouldn't be there when you are brainstorming marketing messages. They don't have the same things to contribute. You get better results when it isn't the same team every day because conversation and personal dynamics tend to be pretty stubborn things. So if you have the same seven people all three days, the way the conversation goes will tend to be relatively predictable. The people who won't speak up in front of the CEO still won't speak up in front of the CEO. And the people who don't get along still won't get along. And it becomes less beneficial to have the same communication patterns every day. So, of those seven people, no more than 4 of them should be in the room every day.

Ideally, I also like to include one person from the outside on Day 3. Someone in the industry who is in a position to understand and know the challenges, the model, and the opportunities. Invite someone as close to a competitor as you are comfortable doing. They will have great insights. But make certain it's someone you trust to be in that meeting.

What to bring

In the next chapter I cover some of the data your team should bring. But here I'm talking about office supplies.

This works best with a flip chart (with the Post-It strips) and at least 4 different colored markers. You'll use them to keep lists of each of the sections listed under days 1, 2, and 3. Keep them posted around the room for easy reference as you go through each day.

You'll also want to have a screen and a laptop in case you need to search something online or bring up the website.

That's it...except for some snacks and drinks for all three days.

Chapter 4: DAY ONE

Ready to dive in? Let's go!

Day one is the unpacking and it starts with a lightning round description of your business, your products, and your sales process. Neither the team nor the facilitator should do any prep for day one. You want to go in with a blank mind and not really know what you are going to be discussing, because it works better as an organic process. One of the interesting things I see when I'm facilitating is the responses when I ask people the question, "What business are you in?" Different people give significantly different answers. Some people might say, for example, "We are in the financial advisory business." Some people might say, "We are in the publishing business." Others will say, "We are in the marketing business." Others will say, "We are an internet marketing business. We are in the email business."

The reason it matters is it helps us reset the focus on the right things. If you consider yourself a financial publisher, for example, is your product available on newsstands? Or do you only sell directly to the consumer online or through the mail? In the former, your business would likely rely heavily on advertising dollars. In the latter, it would rely on your customer acquisition. This would make you more of a marketing business than a publishing one. Asking "What business you are in?", lets you see where the biggest future opportunities are.

Of course, there are some things that you don't want to fly blind on. I always ask that the client brings the following key performance indicators (KPIs):

- Revenue by product or product line in numbers and percentages (You want to know how much something is contributing, but you also want to know what percent it is contributing.)

- Refunds...again, in dollars and percentages. It is extremely important to note if something is contributing a significantly higher percentage of refunds than it is a percentage of revenue because that indicates a problem with the product.

- Number of customers and lifetime value by product and product line are important.

- Cost of goods sold by product

- Bottom line profit by product and product line

- Any other numbers that are critical to your business

For a Business Cleanse, we don't want to spend a lot of time diving deep into these numbers. Having one copy of financials for reference, and having copies of bar and pie charts is my preferred way to review this.

I also ask for a full list of resources. One of the things that people always get stuck on is defining their resources. For most people, they think it's either their products or their customer lists (or both). They don't realize that every source of knowledge you have is a resource. One of the things that we are going to be doing further down the road is looking for new opportunities with new potential partners. I recommend that everybody come with a list of resources that they can use to entice people to do business with them.

Here's an example of what I mean. I had a client who very much wanted to send an offer to somebody else's email list, but she didn't have her own list to reciprocate -- and that is a very standard thing in the industry. You have to have a mailing list the other party can send an offer to. However, she had great connections at QVC and at Whole Foods. I knew this was a unique opportunity. Everyone else could offer them mailing lists. She had something special.

I told her to make the list of people she wanted to do business with and we would let them know that they can get introductions to QVC or Whole Foods -- and she'll be able to give them an opportunity that they wouldn't have otherwise. So even though she didn't have a 250,000 person email list to give them, she has this other resource that is so valuable to them that they didn't have access to any other way.

Anything that is usable in your business or valuable to you is valuable to somebody else. Your list of connections, your marketing knowledge, and your systems knowledge, any of those things can be valuable to the right person.

For the Cleanse, you want your team to bring that list of resources to make sure that you are playing with a full awareness of what you can bring to the table.

Before we talk about the products and product lines, we want to look at the different business units and their year over year growth. Watching these patterns shows where we should invest more in the future and which things used to be significant parts of the business that might have been falling off. It's an opportunity to figure out: is it time to re-invest in them or is it time to move away from them?

That list of areas you should invest more in and the products that have been falling is going to be key in determining the direction of days 2 and 3.

That may seem like a fairly quick day...but it's pretty full.

Regardless of what time you get through Day 1, don't start on Day 2. You can go back and revisit any discussions you tabled, head back to the office, or just head out.

Chapter 5 DAY TWO

Day 2 is when we dissect and destroy. Okay…I'll admit that's a little dramatic, but I like the alliteration and the forcefulness of it. There's nothing tentative about this process. We want it to make impactful decisions that will help your business grow faster and get out of a rut.

STFU

On day 2, after everyone has their coffee and is settled, dive in by creating a "Shut the F Up" list. I realize that, too, sounds a little harsh. Let me explain. The STFU list is the list of things the CEO or partners are non-negotiable about. It doesn't matter if they are draining money, being ignored, dragging down more critical projects, these are off the table. Generally, this list should have no more than a couple things on it (if any!). But if the leader(s) of the company refuse to budge on something, it's not worth making it part of the discussion. Our goal is to streamline, not to complain.

One client had a consultant on retainer that her partner didn't see value in. Every time they would meet to talk about the business, they would spend 30 minutes (at least!) discussing why this consultant hadn't been fired. Simple. It wasn't going to happen. It was the first thing on our STFU list. By taking it off the table, we spent our time looking at other areas of the business where everyone was open to change and opportunities instead of rehashing an old argument.

BEDD – Swatting the SWOT

For years everybody was talking about doing a SWOT Analysis: Strengths, Weaknesses, Opportunities and Threats. At the time it was a very important and useful business tool. But what I found over the years is that, many things we would talk about would end up on three of the four lists. And also, except for opportunities the other three really weren't that valuable for how I was going to move forward the next day. Knowing what my team's strengths were...what my business' strengths were...what our weaknesses were, I basically knew those. And the threats are things that you need to know about, but that you can't really do much about them. In the direct mail business, we would say a threat would be a postage hike. Well, all we could do was sit and wait to see if it was going to happen. Then we would either raise our prices, raise our shipping, or take the hit, but it wasn't going to change how we did business.

Side note: In today's world, the big threat is changes in rules by Google and Facebook. But knowing that doesn't help you plan for it. Millions of companies are still entirely dependent on one of them or Amazon. If you're having success on any of those platforms, start aggressively testing other options (Pinterest, Bing, etc.) so if you lose your ranking or the algorithm changes, you're prepared with a Plan B.

I wanted to make sure that I refocused this on things that would be truly impactful and change the lens of the business. I created a different way of looking at the business for my clients. I call it B-E-D-D, which is Brag, Embarrassed, Dreams and Distractions. I'll go through them now one at a time the way that I work with clients on them. Very much like a SWOT analysis, each of these is a list and this is where your flip chart and your markers are going to come in handy-- make sure you have at least four colors.

BRAG:

Some people think it's a dirty word, but I use it on purpose. There's a level of pride in the things you brag about that is greater than the rest of your business. So...what do you brag about? You can use these questions as a jumping off point:

- What do you love about your business?
- What do you do better than anybody?
- What do you do that makes the competition look at you and say, "Why can't we do this as well as they do?"
- What are the things that your customers call up and thank your customer service team for?
- What are your highest ratings on Amazon?

- What are your best lowest return rates?

- What are the things that you do so well in the business that if somebody came to you and said, "Change this," you would say, "Absolutely not! We are so good at this, don't touch it."

- What are the products that your customers love so much, that you'd be afraid to change them?

EMBARRASSED:

Now weaknesses, everybody has and you can work around them. But what I like to nail down with my clients is what are you embarrassed about?

This can be a tough conversation. People can be a little sheepish at first because they want to pretend everything is awesome and they are Mr. Loyal.

But every company has them. Whether it's a marketing campaign or tactic, slow customer service, products that break, etc. The company I used to work for used some very aggressive political language to sell products and, as it got stronger, I wasn't proud of what we were doing. Once I became embarrassed about it, I decided to leave.

Every company has their embarrassments...every single one.

Here's a list of questions to use to get your team to think about and shout them out:

- What are the things that we feel ashamed of being associated with?
- What would you be embarrassed to put your own name on – and show to your grandmother?
- What do people call customer service complaining about?
- What reviews would you take down from Amazon, Yelp, etc. if you could?
- What would you not want people at a networking event to know you had worked on?

Making those very honest assessments...saying, "This is embarrassing to me. This is embarrassing to our company. We shouldn't do this. I don't want my name associated with this," that is a hard list to make, especially in front of the CEO. It's one of the reasons that the facilitator has to be strong and has to be willing to have the hard conversations, but this list may be the most important. You want to talk about the things you are embarrassed about because those are the things, at the end of the process. that you are going to work to change immediately. Because uncovering what's slowing down your growth, or why you are not as profitable as last year -- those are very easy things to identify and can be fixed. But when people are embarrassed by what you are doing as a company, they will leave, they will sabotage projects, they will even embarrass you if they can, because they feel uncomfortable being associated with your practices.

If something is on the Embarrassed list, make sure that you are very upfront about it and that you are very aggressive about changing them as quickly as you can. You also want to acknowledge them to your employees and be honest if you're not going to change them. You can say things like, "I know that you wish that we didn't operate this way. And now that you've brought it to my attention, I see it, too. But until we can fix XY and Z, this is a very important part of our business. So we are going to commit to changing those things in the next year and move away from this part of our business." If it's not something you can change immediately, at least let people know that you've heard them, you recognize it, you know it's an embarrassment and you don't want it to be part of your business anymore either.

DREAMS:

A lot of people use the word "goals" but that's never worked for me. Even when I was running a $70 million-dollar business, I didn't believe in setting goals. There are two reasons I don't believe in goals.

1) When you set goals for people, they reach them.

If you have a sales team and you tell them that you want them to hit $50,000 a month in sales, how many of them are going to go above $50,000 a month? Probably zero. And even if they get $75,000 in sales one month, they may try to hold back that "extra" $25,000 to make sure they make their goal the next month. If you just say to them "Go as hard, as fast, as long as you can and you'll be rewarded for it," they will probably bring in a lot more than $50,000 that month and every month.

2) Goals make you feel like you have failed when you don't hit them.

Let's say you have that $50,000 goal and somebody hits $48,000, they failed. They didn't make that goal. And maybe in your business you do consider that failure, but would you really want someone that got 96% of their goal to feel like a complete failure? Still let's use another example. Let's use weight loss, I'm somebody who, earlier in my life, was extremely overweight and I took a year and I focused on my weight and I lost 52 lbs. Now if I had set a goal of 60 pounds, 52 would be a failure. I would have struggled. I would have said "I can never lose those last 8 pounds," and I would feel horrible about it. But instead I set a dream that I was just going to be lighter. That I was going to lose as much weight as I could, be as small a size as I could and keep going until I stopped losing weight. So I lost 52 pounds, which was a pretty significant number but it was never a goal.

'Dreams' is a tricky word, because people also always think they are these kind of huge, crazy things. So I like to think of them as attainable dreams. If you are running a $1 million dollar business, don't write down the dream to become a $100 million dollar business in 2 years, but you can dream that you will become a $10 million dollar business.

Here are the questions to ask for the Dreams section:

- What you want your business to be?
- Where you want it to be in the marketplace?
- What competitors to do you want to outperform – and in what area?

- Who you want to do business with that you aren't working with now?
- Who are your dream hires?
- What's the biggest dream you have for your business?

DISTRACTION:

Distractions are often projects or processes that somebody came up with a while ago that no longer serve your business, but for whatever reason you don't get rid of them. Years ago, in my old business, somebody got a body cream sample at a trade show. He son had pretty severe diaper rash and eczema and this product was clearing in up when nothing else could. We were so impressed and decided to license it. We all loved it. It was great for hands, it was great for feet, some people put it on their faces, and everyone on our team who used the cream loved. Except the market. We had a very hard time selling it. The only way we could sell it was a buy one, get one free and we really couldn't afford to do that with our margins. So for years we had kept this product because we all thought it was great. But it wasn't. It was a distraction. It took a long time to produce. The containers for it were difficult to source and had high minimums. There were a lot of moving parts to it, and it wasn't selling. So even though we all loved it, it was really a distraction and it needed to stop being a part of the business.

Identifying those things that are just kind of still around, but they are really not a good use of anybody's time, are very important. In my previous business, a lot of our business was supplements and beauty and there was a rule that any product that couldn't post $50,000 to the bottom line would be killed. I know that sounds like a high number, but on a $70 million dollar business, it's not.

A lot of people asked me why I would be willing to give up $50,000. Because a product that can't make more than that doesn't get attention. Yet, we would still have it on the website, we still had to educate customer service about it, and we still had to make sure the inventory wasn't expired (we only had 2 years to sell the inventory). It was a risk with the FDA and the FTC, if we had an unhappy customer. You can see that every product creates a lot of potential pitfalls, and some don't deserve enough attention for those potential pitfalls. So if it couldn't contribute $50,000, I didn't want to have to focus on it. I also knew that we would have to replace that $50,000. By giving up the money from weak product, you create more opportunity for new products that can grow much bigger.

Now your number might not be $50,000, but figure out what that number is or what that metric is and make it a hardline. That's the beginning of the list of products or projects or business units that should no longer be a part of your company.

Let's play LEGO:

It's time to identify the LEGOs in your business. Yup...we're talking about those feet-killing blocks.

The best way I can describe this is if you've ever played with Lego (and you are not a master. Yes...there are LEGO masters), you've probably just taken a bunch of blocks and put them together. Maybe you say, "I'm going to make a dinosaur," so you put a bunch of blocks together and you look at it and you think, "It looks like a wide building, maybe it just needs a tail." So you put a tail on it and then you look at it and you think, "It kind of looks like a building with a tail. Maybe it just needs a big head." So you put a big head on it and it just looks like a building with a weird-looking tail and something that is probably a head. At this point, no matter what you do, you are never going to turn this long building into a dinosaur. You need to stop trying to make it something else, break it down, and start over.

In business, I think one of the best examples of this is an Excel spreadsheet. Somebody puts together a spreadsheet and then somebody wants to add another payment option, then somebody wants to add another product line that is sold differently. By the end you have this crazy big spreadsheet. Some of the formulas will be wrong, some of the numbers won't make sense in every product, but people just keep adding and adding and tweaking. If you had broken it down and started it over or made it an individual spreadsheet, it would be more manageable, and the numbers would be more accurate.

There are these things that we do all the time in business, where we just keep sticking tails on buildings thinking, "Oh, it just needs this." We do it a lot with our marketing, where instead of killing a piece of bad marketing and starting from scratch, we just keep editing and editing. I used to say, "We spent a lot of time making mediocre stuff less mediocre." If you are sticking stuff on to a spreadsheet, to a marketing campaign, to a product, stop it, knock it down and start over and build it the right way.

Talk to your team about what a LEGO project is, make a list of the ones in your business, and talk about how to break them down and make them work better again.

BATMAN PROJECTS:

These are some of my favorites. I talk a lot about not getting distracted. But I like to make sure we still shoot for the stars.

I mess up this story, but it's still one of my favorite ones. It was an NPR story several years ago about this guy who is blind, but he uses a series of sounds and clicks and does things sighted people are scared to do. He will ride his bike through the middle of town on the street. The reason he rides his bike is because he didn't listen to people who told him he couldn't.

When you see exciting opportunities that you want to test and people say, "Well, we can't really do that because...," you can really do that.

Go back and revisit the things that people told you couldn't do or wouldn't work in your business. Make a list of those projects and products that people convinced you not to try and evaluate them in terms of your business today.

BEGIN AGAIN:

The last thing that we discuss on day two is this question: "If today was day one, knowing everything you know today, what would you do differently?" So all the pitfalls, all the lessons, all the people, what would it look like if you knew all of that and today was day one? Let's start to build THAT company.

At the end of day two, everybody should go get a drink and clear your heads for a big day 3!

Chapter 6 DAY THREE:

Day three is my favorite day because that's when we put all of this into brainstorming and action. On Day 3, we plan the products and the opportunities, and we brainstorm creative ideas. It's also the day that everybody leaves with marching orders. I call day three, "Bring it!"

We start with creative brainstorming. Everyone has their own brainstorming styles and strategies. This is the process I've used for more than 10 years and it's led to tens of millions of dollars in additional revenue.

To get the process started, the first question should be: "What is the biggest promise that we can make about our product or business?"

You want it to be realistic, but you want it to be HUGE. Ignore legal concerns at this stage, you are just brainstorming.

If you have a financial business, it might be 'Retire in one year, no matter how much money you have in the bank now.' Or a health business, 'Never get sick again.' If it's a dog-training businesses, 'Train your puppy to never pee in the house – by tomorrow.'

Whatever is the biggest promise that you could make that you believe you can back up, write that down and focus on it.

From there, here are other questions that will get the ideas flowing:

- What keeps your customers up at night and what do they wake up thinking?

  Nobody ever woke up in the morning and said, 'I wish my joints were better lubricated.' They said, 'I wish my knees didn't hurt so much!'" So think about the experience that your customers are having AND the way they are explaining it.

- If you weren't what you are, what would you be? This one can be a little trickier so let me explain with an example everyone knows: Apple Computers. Everybody knows that Apple products are the hipper, cooler products versus Microsoft. So if you are a new shoe company and you want to be the hip, young company that is going to attract people a little bit on the fringes, instead of the stable, buttoned-up business company, you would compare yourself to Apple, not Microsoft. You can use that as a jumping off point about how to position yourself in the market and what people are looking for and what they care about. With this exercise, I always ask people to think of themselves in terms of a completely different universe. Who would you be in the smartphone universe? Who would you be in the fashion universe? Or in the athletic shoe? Wherever you can say, "In this landscape, we would be this one," it's a great opportunity to figure out how you are positioning your company and it opens up your mind think very, very differently.

- Who is the absolute best at what you do?
- Who is better than you at what you do, and what are they the weakest at?

That is a great way to figure out how to attack competitively. Let me use a football analogy— I love football analogies. If you are a running back and you're constantly running up the middle and coming up against a team who has a tight defensive line, it's just not going to work. You have to look at it differently. They have a solid defensive line, so where is their weakest spot? Who is their weakest blocker? That is where you are going to run.

NEW AGAIN

When you are brainstorming, you are usually trying to come up with new ideas. But some of your best ideas are the things you've already done. Go back to the things that used to work...your old marketing controls, your old campaigns, even your old product launches, and see if you can make them fresh again. Make them new again. Use them again. Because your audience hasn't changed that much. And even though something can get tired, it can also become effective again after a rest.

After the creative brainstorm, move on to new product development. Look at what you are going to add to the product line.

Once you have a list of new product ideas, here are three tips I use to decide which new products to develop:

1. Start with "Hell, no." I'm going to use a supplement example again, because that's where I spent so much of my career. But typically people say, "Let's do a weight loss product." And

everyone would agree, "Cool, let's do a weight loss product. Go find some ingredients and we'll come up with some marketing ideas." And your weight loss product is on its way. But I decided to flip that on its head. When people would suggest a product, I'd respond, "We are not going to make that product. Now convince me that it deserves to be made." By starting from a place of "No," we wouldn't make a product unless someone "fought for its life" and convinced us it should be made – and can be marketed.

2. The next rule is the one-year rule. John Irving, the famous author, says if a character doesn't live in his head for at least ten years, he doesn't write them. Basically, they have to refuse to go away. So anytime you have a product idea, ignore it and see if it sticks around long enough. If it won't go away, it needs to be created. The company that I built is a universal trust badge for the internet economy. The idea is that if you are hiring a babysitter or a dog walker, or renting your house on Airbnb, they can share their SafetyPIN

so you know you can trust them. The first time I had the idea...the kernel of it...was probably three or four years before I launched the business. It evolved and evolved, and it changed, but it wouldn't die. It wasn't an easy thing to put out of my head and say, "I'm never going to do that." You have to make sure that your ideas will fight for their life, because if they don't get excited about themselves, if you can just put it out of your head, it's not going to be an important idea to your audience.

3. The last question I ask in the product development section is: "Okay, now that we have all these products we want to develop, what if you can only keep one of them?" It's the best way to figure out which ones you should do first. So...if you could only keep one, which one of these would you keep?

Earlier I mentioned that you can resurrect old products and test them again. At the same time, it's important to remember that you're not in the product resuscitation business. Remember this: "Dead products don't lie and neither do their sales numbers." You have to know when it's time to pivot and when it is time to just give it up. It can be a very hard thing for business owners to do, but sometimes you just have to.

Prioritizing ideas

This brings us to the heart of the Business Cleanse, the priority grid.

The priority grid helps identify the projects you're going to move on right away and the ones you're going to kill – and those in between.

On the Y axis is "The Cost" and on the X axis is "The Opportunity."

When I say "cost," it's important to understand that I don't just mean money, because money is the easiest resource to replace. Consider what it is going to cost you in terms of time, personnel and even things like a marketing opportunity with a big influencer. In a situation like that you likely only get one chance, so that is a cost. If you use it on the wrong thing, you will never get that opportunity again.

So you want to look at what something is going to cost versus how much opportunity it can bring to your business. The upper left-hand corner represents those products that require a high cost and offer low opportunity. And those are projects that we kill. Yes, kill. We do not back burner them. We do not decide to do them halfway. We kill them and we never discuss them again. They have no place in your business.

On the lower left-hand quadrant are the products that are relatively low cost, but they are not big opportunities. In this quadrant, the rule is, if somebody on your team believes in the project and is willing to champion it (on their own time so it doesn't interfere with their main responsibilities), they get to do this. The product champion gets to bring it to life, and if it works, they should get a significant bonus for it. You need a product champion and they have to be willing to put in extra time and extra hours, and if it turns into what they thought it was going to be, they have a huge upside.

Now on the upper right-hand quadrant are things that are a big investment of resources, but also present a big opportunity. These are the things that you commit to when you have the resources for them. If money is not an issue, hire a consultant as a project manager so that your core people aren't distracted from their primary responsibilities and you have someone dedicated to oversee the project and make it happen, because personnel resources are usually the most limited. Here's an example of something you would put in this quadrant. If you have an online store and you are on WooCommerce and want to move to Shopify, you can see how that would be a significant opportunity in the future. If you want to replace a shopping cart on your website, that is a significant investment, but it's also a huge opportunity. That is a perfect example of something that, when you have the resources, you should do. It's a perfect type of project to bring somebody in from outside who would be able to offer focused attention to it, without distracting from other projects.

Now we have the lower right-hand quadrant. These are things that have relatively minimal investment and need relatively minimal resources and are significant opportunities. So for example, in a direct response business, that could be a new marketing package, a new piece of copy. Relatively low investment, huge opportunity and payoff if it's done well. You can never have more than five items in this quadrant. More than five is too many projects for your overall team. As projects get completed, new projects get moved into the quadrant.

Chapter 7 WHAT HAPPENS

NEXT?

Congratulations! You've spent three days unpacking, uprooting, and preparing your business for growth again.

You've killed fledging projects, brainstormed new marketing and product development, prioritized everything and made your priority grid.

Now is the time for ACTION.

Call the team back together for a kick off meeting.

DEFINING SUCCESS – AND FAILURE

The first thing you need to do is look at the projects in your lower right-hand quadrant and define success and failure. It's important to stick with those definitions. It can be tempting to "grade on a curve" if something comes close, especially when it's a project you support personally. But there are reasons you've chosen these definitions, so commit to them.

In my old business we used a measure of "revenue per name" as a measure of success in our direct mail campaigns. Typically, 60 or 70 cents per name would be a very, very good return. We had one product that was doing fairly well to new customers, but they weren't renewing well and they weren't buying other products from us. So where normally we would look for a $0.60 to $0.70 per name return in a direct mail campaign, we did the math and realized that we would need $1.25 in order to continue this product.

We developed a new marketing piece. That piece brought in $1.05 per name and I shut the newsletter down.

The owners of the company came to me and they said, "But you got $1.05 per name, that's amazing. That's almost double what we normally do and it's remarkable. We usually do $0.60 and you did $1.05. That campaign is a huge success!"

"But we need $1.25," I said. And they couldn't get over the fact that as an absolute, $1.05 was a great number, but because of the low renewal rate, the low product ordering rate, and the low advertising income we were getting from these customers, we needed to bring in $1.25 from every new customer. So even though $1.05 on its face seems like a great success, it wasn't.

I had defined what failure was and I honored it.

You must define those numbers. You have to draw lines in the sand. They have to be firm. And you have make a commitment that if something succeeds, it succeeds and if it fails, it fails. It's important as a leader that your team sees that you are sticking to these decisions, even if it's your own project. Even if it's your own idea. That's when it's the hardest to say, "Well, it did $1.05, maybe we can give it another chance?" You absolutely cannot do that, you have to stick to these metrics.

ASSIGNING CHAMPIONS

Next, you assign the product champions to all of the projects that you are moving forward on now -- primarily those that are in that lower left-hand and right-hand quadrants — the projects that offer the best opportunities, and the ones that need their own product champion to survive.

Make sure the people leading the top 5 projects are thought leaders and great at delegation. You don't want them to become bottlenecks in making things happen because they keep too much on their own plates.

Then you allocate the financial resources necessary to make it happen. If you haven't read 'Lean Startup,' you should. I operate in lean startup mode all the time, whether I was running a $70 million dollar business or a business that is barely making $7,000. Either way, if you operate the business as a lean startup, you are always doing the things that your business needs for success and you don't have to pullback and readjust where you are spending and how.

DAILY HUDDLE

Once you have project champions in place and resources allocated, schedule a daily huddle with either the whole team or the different project-based teams. It should be just be 10 or 15 minutes. The important thing about these meetings is they are not status meetings. It is not for somebody to read their to-do list or to justify their job. The things that happen in this conversation are big wins that the whole team can celebrate, or" I need help with X" or "I can help with X." That is the purpose of this. It's a 'Where are we? What needs to be done? What do you need help with? How do we help?' kind of call. It's not an 'I am still working on getting the homepage of the website live." We all know that everyone there is doing a job and that they are bringing value, if they are not, that's a different conversation. So for the people that are on that team, you have to give them the comfort that the point of this discussion is not to defend their presence, but to help where they can help and to get help where they need it

STAFFING DECISIONS

Maybe the most difficult part for people is the honest, somewhat raw look at staffing. Personally, I have an easy way of deciding who to keep and who to let go. I ask myself, "If the person walked into my office and resigned today, would I panic and offer them more money to stay? Or would I thank my lucky stars because now I never have to fire them, and I am thrilled that they are leaving and leaving on their own terms?" If it is the latter and I am thrilled that the person is leaving, then actually I have to fire them because if I would be relieved for them to go, I have to let them go.

Identify who those people are and figure out an exit plan for them. Figure out a time to implement it. And even though you may feel like they do 'enough' and you feel bad and don't really know if you should fire them, you should. My solution is always be more generous with severance then you need to be and make it as easy for them as possible. Be squarely focused on making sure the person you're letting go has as seamless of an exit as possible.

It's going to suck no matter what. Firing people generally sucks.

Early in my career I did this very, very badly. There was somebody who I gave them far too little severance. I was given misdirection by one of the leaders of my company and instead of giving the person fair severance, they invested in a career coaching program for her. Instead of giving her the money and saying, "We found these programs, and if you'd like to try one, you should." It was a thing I was very ashamed about. The person came back to the company several years later in a different role. I apologized several times and said, "I think you are the most significant professional mistake I ever made. I was not fair to you." Assuming your company can afford it and you're not firing for specific cause, make sure that you are giving people more severance than you think you should. It is the best money you can invest. It's relatively few dollars, gives you peace of mind, lets the employee transition easier, and – if they talk about, which people often do – it makes you look better to your remaining employees.

As a side note, I have a very simple script that I use when I'm letting somebody go. Anytime I bring this up when I'm speaking, everyone makes me repeat multiple times so they can write it verbatim. This is obviously a huge sticking point for people.

It's intentionally short and it intentionally shares minimal information because usually once you start talking, you get yourself in trouble with something as significant as termination.

Here is my script in its entirety:

"I want to thank you for everything you've done for the company to date. I've decided that you are not one of the people that is going to help us move the company forward and I've decided to let you go."

Then I tell them whomever is going to help with their human resources and their COBRA, getting their keys back, etc. and I leave the room. It's important that you do not fire people in your own office. You want to be able to walk out of the room. It's also very important that you thank the person for what they've done if you choose to, but that you don't say, "You've done a great job." those are two very different things and in some states saying the phrase, "You've done a great job," can actually put you in a legal predicament. So it's thanking them for what they've done, but not putting a value on it.

Now back to the scenario where someone came in and resigned today. We've talked about what to do if you'd be relieved. Now what about if you would panic and want to throw money at them?

First, think what that number would be. If the person came in and said, "I got an offer paying me $10,000 more," would you match it? Would you increase it? Whatever the number is that you would either match or that you would increase it to, go give that person that money today. Because a) they will stop looking for a job, b) they won't be open to a job if a recruiter contacts them and c) they will feel so incredibly valued, it will knock their socks off.

If you don't want to do it as salary, do it as a bonus, but I recommend that you do it as salary. If you really, really wouldn't want to lose them, pay them now to make them stay and to make them incredibly loyal.

In addition to that litmus test for who you should let go and who you should make feel valuable, another way I assess staff is meeting participation. To me, meeting participation is not a right. It's a privilege that you have to earn. If you don't participate in meetings, you don't get invited. And if you don't get invited and you can't participate, you miss further opportunity to show your value. I also assess people based on how they participate in meetings. I invite people in the beginning and they kind of have to earn their right to stay.

In marketing copy we used something called 'The Four U's", which is: Useful, Unique, Urgent and Ultra Specific. I use that to assess employees' participation and in their reviews.

- Useful: Is what they are doing useful? If not, you shouldn't even have the job in your organization, regardless of the person.

- Urgent: What is your sense of urgency like? If something has to be done quickly, do you roll up your sleeves and do whatever you need to make it happen, but not act like Chicken Little and go into a panic?

- Unique: What do they bring to the job that we would not have if they weren't here? What do you they do better than anybody? What is a special skill that you have?

- Ultra Specific: What is something (or several things)

that they personally have done to increase your top and bottom lines or make your business better or move your business forward?

Those are the assessment tools that I use to decide who is going to be a part of my team moving forward and who is not going to be.

GETTING STARTED:

Here are some key things that you can do today. I know that it can be daunting to think about taking three full days with key people. It's a big investment of time. It's an investment of money. And it's also an intimidating process, because you have to be ready to follow through on it. There is no benefit to just bringing your people into this process, hiring a facilitator, going off site for three days, and then shrugging and going back to what you've done before. So take these steps immediately.

1. **Use The Priority Grid**. Determine the products/projects that you know should be killed. Don't even worry about the three other quadrants right now, just the things that take a lot of resources and don't contribute a lot to the business. Put those

in that quadrant and make a plan to kill them FAST.

2. **Determine The Minimum Contribution** or Investment For Each Product In Order To Fight For Its Own Life.

3. **Identify the People That You Would Absolutely Hate to Lose** and review their compensation and then give them the raise (or bonus) that you would give them if they came in and told you they were quitting. If your company has shares or options, you can also give them a new compensation structure that includes that or

increase the amount that they get of that.

4. **Identify The People That You Would Be Relieved If They Came Into Your Office And Resigned Today.** If you are not ready to fire them, that's okay. Just make the list. Make it on a secret document on your phone, but make the list and start the process in your head of weeding out the people that are not contributing to your business in the way that you require.

5. **Choose Somebody On Your Team To Plan The 3-Day Cleanse.** Have them pick the

dates for it and start looking for the location. Just find somebody who is going to be in charge of making it happen and let them start planning it. They can look for a facilitator. They can suggest who should be in the room which days. But make sure that somebody on your team is primarily responsible for the planning of it, so that you are committed to the process moving forward.

CONCLUSION

A 3-Day Business Cleanse is a big commitment – of time, resources, money, and talent. Before scheduling one, make sure you are committed to implementing the changes that arise from it.

This is an opportunity to reset your business with fresh focus and renewed energy...

To move on from areas that aren't building your brand...

To get new insights and ideas from people that aren't always in the conversation...

To re-assess who is (and isn't) contributing to your company and realign responsibilities to get the most from your best people...

To end relationships with employees that aren't capable or willing to move the business forward...

To get your team to rally behind the 5 biggest opportunities in front of you...

To take your business off of auto-pilot and fly some loop-de-loops...

And so much more...

So if you've been feeling "stuck," frustrated, bored, or behind the 8-

ball, it's time to bring people together, plan a 3-Day Business Cleanse, get the sh*t out of your business, and get things moving again.

Here's to your success!

Facilitator notes

If you're going to be running a 3-Day Business Cleanse for a client, here are some critical points to consider:

1) As I mentioned earlier, you should not be looking to turn this into an ongoing consulting opportunity. Doing so will make you far less likely to push back on leadership regarding pet projects, trouble employees, etc. Go in thinking "This is a 3-day commitment and that's all I am here for." If a longer-term opportunity presents itself after the fact,

there's no reason you can't take it. But this shouldn't be the jumping off point for getting yourself a new gig.

2) Facilitating this meeting can be tough. You have to push and drill down...trying to get to the real challenges and issues. Watch the body language and the relationships between people. I was once in a meeting where a screaming match broke out and people started crying. Even though the CEO/leader is there, you are responsible for controlling the room. That means shutting down any yelling immediately,

managing disagreements, and cutting off discussions that aren't productive.

3) If you know the industry or are a consumer of the product, you can contribute ideas or comment on theirs. Otherwise, your role should be strictly facilitation.

4) At the end of each day, I have someone from their team photograph all the notes taken (as do I) and I take the notes back to my hotel to transcribe. You want to do this yourself and while it's still fresh. You'd be surprised how little sense your own notes make 2-3 days

later. I literally just transcribe what's there and add a little more detail where necessary. This is the bulk of the deliverable to the client, presuming they've been taking notes and making plans throughout.

5) Make sure you are charging the client enough that they feel like they have already invested in the process. Otherwise, it's easy for them to go back to the status quo. It's the one time I'm in favor of the Sunken Costs idea. If they believe they have to proceed on some things because they already invested

$X, good things will happen. It's like hiding peas in the mashed potatoes. You're making sure they do what's good for them – or rather their business.